CW00956850

POETRY
OF A
GEISHA

BY

ELIZABETH ITŌ

Copyright©ElizabethItō2022
All rights reserved.
ISBN: 9781549975707
Copyright©ElizabethItō2022

These chosen moments,
each memory now long passed…
now recalled with joy.

FOREWORD

Of a life lived in servitude...

To many, the thought of an existence solely intent on the pleasing of others may seem strange if not terrifying, yet as I hope to portray within the pages of this book, the confining moments of my position as a geisha and different stages required to reach such standings were to be cherished.

There is often a confused outlook on a chosen profession of hostess and sponsored paramour. A mystery presented in the true reasoning behind a want to live a life at the beck and call of others, the answers of which can be found hidden within the complexities of selfless service to another.

In a range of differing scenarios, from those of horseplay and mere flattery, to the more intimate surroundings found in pleasures sought within the company of another soul, it is in the sheer act of duty towards another that a provider's own pleasured rewards reside.

For there are two realms at rule inside the arenas of geishahood, for not only can a certain beauty be found in subservience, there can also be a great capacity for power and dominance over those a geisha is paid to adhere to.

It is in this equilibrium of both passive and dominant roles that leads to understanding the complexities of what it truly means to be of service, to submit one's self to others on a daily basis within an often chosen scale of years.

From a geisha's beginnings as a Shikomi maid, and within the advancement of apprenticeship seen in a Minarai and Maiko's trials, awareness behind each role taken becomes apparent, resulting in said pleasures received from submitting to the obedience of others.

This is the reasoning behind my words.

A want inherent within me to tell of an enigmatic life lived in dutiful submissiveness, and to express what has been encountered on my own voyage upon the oceans of a geisha's calling.

Elizabeth Itō
Zurich, Switzerland

Contents

Part One

An Apprentice   11

The Okiya   13
Shikomi   21
Minarai   29
Onee-san   37

Part Two

Becoming   45

Maiko   47
Hanami-Koji Street   55
Kimono   63
In Preparation   71

Part Three

Geisha   79

Of Entertaining   81
Hanami   89
Arashiyama Bamboo Forest   97
Of Emotions   105

About the Author   113

That rush of senses,
in expressions of service.
A story begins.

AN APPRENTICE

Freshness of being,
beginnings of paths ahead.
Keenness of duty.

THE OKIYA

SHIKOMI

MINARAI

ONEE-SAN

THE OKIYA

Traditionally constructed in wood from locally sourced forestlands, an Okiya is the house in which a geisha lives for the entirety of her profession.

Run and managed by an Okā-san, the Japanese name for mother, it is she who sees to the majority of expenses acquired by residing geishas and apprentice Shikomi, Maiko and Minarai. These outlays include paying for kimonos and for the training of all novices in the art of becoming a fully-fledged geisha.

A geisha's career, nenki, begins with first being accepted into the Okiya, where in their new home they train under the watchful eye of their Okā-san, who in later years may adopt one of her trained geisha as a musume, daughter, in view of becoming an Atotori, the eventual heiress of her Okiya.

Living within the Okiya and and working in an adjoining Ochaya, tea house, a geisha performs her trade in hosting skills towards given clients, which include music, dance, talk laughter and the inevitable partaking of alcohol.

As reimbursement of her training and lodging, a qualified geisha gives a percentage of her earnings to her Okā-san in order to maintain the house and support all others living in the Okiya, these include any apprentice geisha who may be present as well as retired geisha, house maids and servants.

Of First Arrivals

Behind a doorway of lacquered black sheen,
entrance to years ready to unfold,
a tentative step forward.

Footfalls taken in wonder
along pathways of instruction…

An apprentice's voyage commences
in lessons of servitude to others.

Finding Place

Chaotic yet still,

this contrast of moments

within a home anew.

To hear laughter and call

of elder sister's delight...

To find peace

contained by secluded Okiya garden walls.

A balance of emotions...

these required elements

in keen retaining of heart.

Okiya doorways.
A knock, a bow, an entrance...
Desires held within.

Of lacquered access,
openings to those of means
for unveiled pleasures.

SHIKOMI

Translated into English as 'preparation', Shikomi is the title given to a novice geisha on first entering an Okiya.

Although a geisha in training, a Shikomi is primarily seen as a maid to the Okiya, with duties of running errands, cleaning and seeing to the preparation of an Ochaya ready for visiting clients. It is in this stage of a geisha's career that her tutors are resolved in the making or breaking any young woman who enters the Okiya with proposed aims of one day becoming a geisha.

Alongside their chores of keeping the Okiya clean and tiny, a Shikomi attends classes in a Hanamachi geisha school, where under the tuition of former geishas and those adept in areas of music, dance and ceremony, a young novice learns of the talents needed in becoming a geisha.

It is during this time that a novice is instructed in playing the shamisen, a three-stringed, long necked instrument that is strummed with a large pick, which is played at parties and is often accompanied by the singing of another geisha.

During these music lessons a Shikomi may also learn to play other Japanese traditional instruments such as another stringed instrument, the koto, a small drum, the shimedaiko, and a type of flute called the fue.

In addition to her duties within the Okiya, the youngest of the household's Shikomi are required to wait up for the Okiya's most senior geisha to return from their evening engagements.

Often returning to the Okiya in the early hours of the morning, it is the Shikomi's duty to aid their elder geisha in removing her kimono, white makeup and brush out the elaborate hairstyle, all trademarks of her future career.

To progress to her next level of becoming a geisha, a Shikomi must be adept within each geisha art, with the passing of a dancing exam seen as the successful completion of her novice years.

Understanding to the Calling

Stages in training,

adhering willingly

to the wants of others…

This servitude resigned

to geisha and geiko of experience;

these elder sisters

of requested demands.

A rite of passage,

relief in awareness to such reasonings,

… so bringing compassion

to all proceedings.

An understanding of need

for chores and duties given.

Reflections of Duty

In simple kimono,

hair tied back in basic of knots.

No makeup present

to hide cheeks flushed crimson

in reddened blush...

A reflection caught in time,

across newly polished tiles of Okiya floor.

Assistance at hand,
in service of others.
Passing rites of all.

In chores of duty,
ceremonies found within.
A polished floor shines.

MINARAI

The life of a Minarai is a quiet one.

Following a novice geisha's successful completion as a Shikomi, she is relieved of her duties and chores of cleaning within the Okiya so she may focus fully on her geisha training. This further training is set within the arenas of geisha life, where a Minarai will observe all proceedings in utmost silence.

Attending her Okiya's ozashiki, banquets and ceremonies attended by those paying for a geisha's services, a Minarai will not participate in any of the rituals performed, instead watching at the side of an elder geisha sister.

In silence, her observations of all surrounding in ways of music, dance and the telling of stories in view of entertaining clients is seen as training for the day she herself will submit such skills to others.

Compensating for the lack of interjection in ceremonial events, the kimono of a Minarai is of elaborate and colourful design, its beauty of cut and finery intended to do all the talking for them.

A geisha's stage of being a Minarai is often a brief one depending on the advancing talents of the individual.

Yet the lack of participation within the many parties and ceremonies a Minarai may attend is seen as vital to her training, with a belief hood running back for centuries that the best way to learn is through the witnessing of others. A schooling which provides the knowledge and awareness of another's needs and emotions made possible by quiet observation.

Revealed Rewards

Advancement from chores to duty…

A time of new worlds
viewed in awe of beauty held.

Attainment of wants revealed.
Remaining silent
a degree of ambitions
yet to be realised.

So emerges those plans,
the schemes and ploys
of how to reach such heights…

To be granted all presented.

Emergence of the Seductive Self

In quiet passing…

A look

a stare,

a blush from attentions given.

The tilt of chin,

underplaying coyness of gaze…

So comes the beginnings of charm,

a novice's shyness evolving into an expert's charisma.

Skills unveiled,

brought forth from theory and into practice.

A time of silence,
watching, listening of mind
amid enticements.

Study of others,
chosen moments of appeal.
To become the lure.

ONEE-SAN

When the stages of being a Shikomi and then a Minarai are complete, a geisha in training must find themselves a Onee-san when entering her next phase of tuition seen in becoming a Maiko.

Viewed as an elder sister, a novice's Onee-san is an older geisha usually from the same Okiya in which previous stages have been reached.

A Onee-san will continue the guidance also seen in the training of a Minarai, with further tuition in acts of tea ceremonies and traditional dance as well as in becoming highly skilled in ways of music and conversation.

To bind the passage from to Minarai to Maiko and ultimately to form a bond between them and their Onee-san, a young trainee geisha will perform the San San Kudo ritual with her elder sister.

The tradition of San San Kudo requires each woman to drink sake from three sake cups. Taking three sips from each cup, the drink is shared with the one you are being bound to, as seen as teacher and student being brought together in unity as one.

This tradition of the bonding of two women is often performed in public at a theatre of banquet and is often then followed by a private party within the confines of the Okiya.

Mentor of Heart

In physicalities of form
a beauty unparalleled.

A chosen mentor…
Not just in standings of appearance;
another quality shines.
A glowing radiance of call…

This option of tutor,
a choice made wisely
in view of
a good heart's welcome.

For an Eager Soul

To stand alone,

to be free…

To leave a teacher's side.

A hush from guiding lips…

reassurance given in soft tones,

in understanding of impatient wants.

"Be still, there is no rush"

a gaze from teacher to student dawns.

"Enjoy all you see…

Enjoy the burning anticipation I see within you."

An apprentice's nod prompts more…

"Soon, young Maiko. Soon."

A mentor of sorts,
leader to hidden delights,
escort for the pure.

Innocence of view,
this elder sister in kind.
Guidance of virtues.

PART TWO

BECOMING

Of knowledge attained,
needs of expression sated
displayed in action.

MAIKO

HANAMI-KOJI STREET

KIMONO

IN PREPARATION

MAIKO

Usually aged between 15 to 20 years old, the final stage of becoming a geisha is that of a Maiko.

As with their previous position of Minarai, a Maiko attends banquets and functions in the Hanamachi flower town areas where geishas live and work, this time at the constant side of her Onee-san.

Sometimes lasting for several years it is in this concluding stage of an apprentice geisha's training that a Maiko's teaching comes principally from lessons taught by her elder sister. Accompanying her Onee-san to all public and private engagements, a Maiko learns the intricacies of a geisha's arts from her mentor.

A Onee-san's teaching is vital. With tutorials on the complexities of tea ceremonies, dancing and the art of conversation, a Onee-san will also help a Maiko in choosing her professional name.

A Maiko will commonly attend morning classes to polish off their talents in the traditional Japanese disciplines of kyomai dances, the playing of music, and in the learning of Kyō-kotoba, the dialect of Kyoto, a necessity required of a Maiko no matter of a her origins. A Maiko's evenings are reserved for working beside her Onee-san so she may practice and hone her skills.

Echoing her time as a Minarai, a Maiko wears a distinct kimono. With long sleeves and a padded hem to create weight and allowing the kimono to trail elegantly on the floor behind her, a Maiko's hikizuri style kinomo denotes her position of being in the closing chapter of a geisha's apprenticeship.

As with the traditions held in a Maiko's appearance and so identification of the stage a trainee geisha has reached, a Maiko will wear many diverse types of nihongami, traditional Japanese hairstyles.

Only visiting a specialised hairdresser once a week, this means in order to maintain their style a Maiko must sleep on a takamakura, a wooden block with a pillow. Depending on the rank of a Maiko within her Okiya, and to the formality need for chosen occasions, a Maiko will use their own hair and not a wig which they decorate with kanzashi, traditional hair ornaments of silver and gem.

In Awareness of Soon Becoming

So a time comes,

when the leaving of all

becomes true.

A day awaited

dreamt of in guise of a kimono's beauty.

These wants to be accepted,

to hold a similar command once shrouded over self.

A kiss of liberty established…

freedom of movement

yet a censorship of speech.

A restraint is held,

lessons still to be learnt acknowledged

made apparent at a consort's side.

Mindfulness of Impatience

This granted chance to perform,
to show those met skills learnt.

A holding back of unsated wants,
a watchful eye reins down
restraint given from a Onee-san's stare.

An accompanied smile
subtle in its experienced turn,
given in awareness to desired displays.

Understandings held within…
Let it unfold,
make their waiting reach its height..
Then Maiko,
the rewards will be yours.

Recitals of heart,
portrayals in song and dance.
A secluded reach.

To play, to perform,
so to remain unattached.
Obscurity, peace.

HANAMI-KOJI STREET

Beside the flowing waters of the Kamo River in the Gion district of Kyoto in the city's eastern reaches, Hanami-koji Street is lined with traditional Japanese wooden machiya houses.

With narrow porticoes measuring only five to six meters wide, Okiya and Ochaya tea houses stand beside restaurants serving Kyoto style kaiseki ryori, Japanese haute cuisine.

It is within these establishments where geiko, the Kyoto dialect for geisha and their Maiko apprentices entertain.

Exclusive and traditionally requiring an introduction from an existing customer to the Okiya, geiko, geisha and Maiko are highly trained and expert hostesses who perform traditional music and dance accompanied by light conversation, serving drinks and the leading of drinking games.

Seen as a popular tourist attraction, Hamani-koji Street offers kimono's for hire to those desiring to walk in the footsteps of the famed geiko's of Gion.

Generations of Footsteps

Zōri shoes,

wooden footfalls

following steps of ages passed.

Remnants of a geiko's duty

granted in echoes of previous times.

So too…

a Maiko's trail,

an apprentice's pathway

across cobble stone lanes.

No different to those of centuries ago.

Within Wooden Walls

A flanking of seclusion
behind polished wood façade
and lacquered door.

Each building a home,
a geisha's lodging,
a Shikomi's dream.

Amid a setting of work and respite,
within a samisen's chord…
long forgotten laughter
embedded into every paper screen,
nestled atop tatami mat
highlighted beneath a lantern's shine.
These continuations of ancient ritual
and desired traditions.

Cobblestone recall,
a walk of wooden shuffles.
A geisha's footfalls.

Distinguished of step,
awaiting payment for smiles
of a client's joy.

Kimono

Learning to carry herself with grace is a customary necessity in becoming and being a geisha.

With poise and elegance, it is of great importance that its wearer walks without tripping over a trailing hemline, or that a kimono's sleeve does not dip into ceremonial cups for either tea or sake.

Meaning 'thing to wear' – ki 'wear' - mono 'thing', the adornment of a kimono is not only the uniform of a geisha or those aspiring to be, but also a garment that is viewed within Japanese society as clothing of formal style associated with politeness and being of good manners.

Distinct to all kimonos, its T-shaped, straight-lined robes are worn so that the hem falls to the ankle, with long wide sleeves and attached collars.

Wrapped around the body, always with the left side over the right, except when dressing the dead for burial, a kimono is secured by an obi, a sash which is tied at the back.

Wrapped around the body, always with the left side over the right, except when dressing the dead for burial, a kimono is secured by an obi, a sash which is tied at the back.

Traditionally made of hemp, linen, silk, silk brocade and satin weaves, the kimono and obi are also widely available in less-expensive easy-care fabrics such as rayon, cotton sateen, cotton, polyester and other synthetic fibres, although silk is still considered to be the most ideal fabric.

Generally worn with traditional footwear of zōri or geta, a kimono is complete with the wearing of tabi, split-toe socks.

Historically, kimonos were taken apart as separate panels for washing and then re-sewn by hand, and old kimonos are often recycled to make haori, hiyoku, kimonos for children.

A Kimono's Call

Of poise,

of give grace.

A kimono's governance…

an expression of standing

of dedications unimagined.

Upturn of collar,

shortening of sleeve,

significance found in discipline and strength.

Secreted awareness towards those of asking…

Understandings reached

in an adornment of colour and finesse of tailored cloth.

Obi of Hidden Treasures

A sash of confinement,

this cumbersome bind.

A constrictment of movement

viewed in delight

of a client's want of dominance…

to keep a lithe figure bound,

wrapped tight in denial of liberty.

Desires confirmed in ritual,

in traditional scenes of servitude.

The kimono…

a uniform of the submissive.

Yet within such restraints a control is held.

For is it not the wearer, she of demure appearance,

the one who guides events now?

Is it not she who decides a ceremony's course?

Controlled seductions towards another,

her prize enclosed taut by an obi of denied releasing.

Encased within folds,
of a Kimono's penance.
A litheness concealed.

Echoed calls of want.
Eagerness of unwrapping.
Seductions begin.

In Preparation

Around twenty to twenty-one years of age, a Maiko is promoted and becomes a geisha in her own right.

This important moment of a geisha's life is marked by the ceremony of 'erikae' to signify the transformation from apprentice to an expert in their chosen field of expertise.

Erikae literally means 'turning of the collar', an expression which identifies a Maiko's passing into being that of a geisha or geiko.

The erikae ceremony is recognised as when a new geisha begins to wear a white collard kimono and so replacing the red collars worn by any young woman of apprentice standing.

To accompany the outward physical appearance of a geisha's new life and the leaving behind of her Shikomi, Minarai and Maiko days, so too does a geisha's hairstyle change from a trainee's ofukyu style to the shimada way, as worn by older Japanese women.

Even though paid in her time of working as a geisha in waiting, a Maiko's advancement into the world of geishadom is marked by an increase in funds given for her services.

With a percentage of her wage going towards the upkeep of the Okiya she still lives within, a popular geisha can become wealthy, with her time with clients measured by the time it takes for an incense stick to burn fully. This traditional ancient way of timekeeping is called 'hanadai' which means 'flower fees'.

When hired to attend parties and gatherings, a geisha's company is called upon in her Okiya tea house, Ochaya, or at within a traditional 'ryotei', a traditional Japanese restaurants.

Customers make arrangements through a kenban, a geisha office, which keeps a geisha's timetable and makes her engagements with paying clients in view of entertaining.

Relief From Willingness

A lifetime's preparing,

arrangement of procedures

honed and ready.

Burning eagerness,

this want of performing for all.

A naivety found in willingness to please.

Innocence of gaze

coupled with belief in all encountered…

A respite found after years of service,

that waits patiently in the wings.

A comfort never before perceived,

when nestling into cynicism's warm hold.

Of Granted Satisfactions

Fresh roads ahead,

a want of travel amid the footsteps of many,

these fearless assignations within arenas new.

This need for performance,

these wants to display talents refined…

A limbo state of forgotten moments,

held within the heart of its portrayer,

an allowance of self given

in hope of a voyeur's praise.

In degrees of wait,
a summit of all knowledge.
Readiness of haste.

Of long drawn out paths;
unveiling of awareness
within completion.

GEISHA

Sculptured blue black sheen,
framing white powdered allure,
glimpsed within repose.

OF ENTERTAINING

HANAMI

ARASHIYAMA BAMBOO

FOREST

OF EMOTIONS

OF ENTERTAINING

The heart of a geisha's duties is that of entertaining others.

After several years and sometimes a lifetime of training and devotion to their craft, a geisha performs and pleases their clientele with a variety of skills and disciplines.

Ozashiki, geisha gatherings, are banquets where when the festivities of eating and drinking are completed a number of geisha take to the stage and perform the sophisticated dance steps and musical instrument playing they are famed for.

An Ozashiki banquet's more formal setting is in contrast to the intimate ceremonies held within a geisha's Ochaya tea room, where sat upon traditional tatami matting, a geisha implements her talents of endearing conversation and storytelling.

Often accompanied by another geisha, both women entertain their clients with renditions by shamisen, dancing and singing. These performances are more often than not complemented by a variety of drinking games.

As to keep their clients from becoming bored, a geisha has a large repertoire of Ozashiki Asobe, party games, to choose from. Most games are played with props, the loser of which is usually required to drink alcohol or do something embarrassing in penalty. As the drinks continue to flow a geisha exerts her authority and makes the games harder, as so does she increase the punishments given of drinking forfeiture.

With Konpira fune fune and Tosenkyo being popular drinking games involving music, quick wits and rounds of sake, a favoured game to be played by clients and geisha alike is Tora, tora, tora.

Translated as Tiger, Tiger, Tiger, and an elaborate version of rock, paper, scissors, a Samurai, an old woman and a Tiger replace the game's namesake.

After a song is sung a geisha and her client then take on the role of one of the three. A winner is announced to the rules of; the old woman beats the Samurai with her cane, but loses to the tiger that eats her, only for the Samurai to cut down the tiger with his sword.

In Ploy of Talk

Laughter in another,

a haunt of joy

arriving in spirited glee.

A call

a tease of words,

a pull on the senses…

Heart strings played upon,

planned to evoke youth hood's freedom.

In Want of Service

A gathering…

these moments of show,

these instances of appearance.

Each woman present

a want within them to delight,

to perform the utmost of her abilities.

A need to satisfy…

born from years of training

in subjection and submission.

Enticements of wants,
controlled given affections.
Endearing pursuits.

Downward tilt of chin,
a raise of seductive eyes.
True objectives gained.

HANAMI

From the end of March to early May, cherry blossom trees bloom across Japan.

Known as Hanami, 'flower viewing'- hana 'flowers' - mi 'to see or view', the occasion is seen in Japanese traditional custom as enjoying the transient beauty of flowers.

With the spectacle being many centuries old, the custom of Hanami is believed to have begun during the Nara period of 710–794, when it was the ume, plum blossoms, that people admired in their masses.

By the Heian period of 794–1185, Hanami became more synonymous with the pink displays of cherry blossom – sakura. A main difference between the two portrayals of springtime arrival is not only in that of colour and timing, but also in scent.

Whereas the pink splendour of cherry blossom has none if any scent at all, is the crop of plum blossom several weeks previous which held the sweet scents which can still linger in the weeks following their demise.

Adopting the practice of Hanami, the Emperors of the Heian period held flower-viewing parties, of which all were plied with sake and rich banquets beneath the pink delicate petals of sakura trees.

Originally limited to the elite of the Imperial Court, Hanami soon spread into samurai society. By Japan's Edo period, the act of welcoming spring's arrival of cherry blossom in ways of feasts and merriment was also held by all within the general population of Japanese society.

As well as announcing Japan's rice-planting season, Hanami was originally was used to divine that year's harvest. Those believing spirits lived inside the trees of sakura made offerings of amongst other items, sake, in hope of a good crop.

Hanami can signal a busy time for a working geisha, as her services are often called for in the guise of accompanying those of wealth and means beneath a canopy of cherry blossom parklands.

Sakura's March

In balance,

a springtime's epoch…

Given collections of pinks;

pure white dashes

cast across open skies

in backdrops of blue.

Splendour in displays observed.

Row upon row

of April's early march

over Japan's eastern seaboard.

A welcoming advance

of never forgotten beauty.

Solely For Others

Accompaniment of clients,

a geisha's calling…

to walk beside a man of means

beneath branches filled with Spring's markings.

His eyes never truly upon his escort,

this rented concubine

of black sheen hair,

powdered white cheeks

and shyness of stare.

Nor a substantial glance

to pink petal myriads above.

Only does he look to others

so they may see who walks beside him,

so they may become aware of his wealth…

shown in the submissive company he keeps.

One year to come,
greeted with harsh March winds.
A short Hanami.

Delicate embrace.
A charged warmth hangs in the air
over pink blossom.

ARASHIYAMA BAMBOO FOREST

With temples scattered across the steep banks of forest hillsides overlooking the Togetsukyo Bridge and the waters of Ōi River, the area of Arashiyama has been a popular destination since first discovered by nobles and dignitaries of Japan's hierarchy of the Heian Period (794-1185).

Against the backdrop of lush, green stems and besides the tranquil grounds of the Fushimi-Inari-Taisha Shrine and Kinkaku-ji Temple, red torii gates mark the entrance to Arashiyama's Bamboo Forest, a labyrinth of walkways over shadowed by the gentle sway of towering bamboo trunks.

Soaring above intimate pathways, the tall, thick bamboo stalks that make up Arashiyama's Sagano Bamboo Forest cast shards of muted sunlight onto those walking beneath towering archways of green.

Swaying in the soft breezes drifting across from the Ōi River, Sagano's gigantic stems creak and rasp in these light winds as they gently collide and twist together, each bamboo stalk accompanied by the rustle of matured leaves set high above the ground.

This distinct rustling adds to the atmosphere of being encircled by Sagano's surreal landscape, so much so that the Japanese Ministry of Environment included the Sagano Bamboo Forest on its list of '100 Soundscapes of Japan', a selection of sounds intended to encourage the people of Japan to stop and enjoy the music in nature.

Seen within Japanese culture as a symbol of strength, bamboo forests are often complemented by Shinto shrines and Buddhist temples, the location of which signifies the warding off of unwanted spirits.

A Stillness

Winding breezes,

accentuated creaks

above and around.

A stillness taken

in the touch of two stems…

Nature's laughter by human design.

In Rays of Sun

Archways,
towering green staffs
of thickened strength.

Walkways of silence
below mighty stem…
bringing tranquillity
of mind and spirit
to all who pass beneath

… highlighted in afternoon sunbeam,
enclosed in comfort.

A change of breeze,
winding between each stalk tier.
Sways of gentle peace.

Ribbed landscapes of green,
great strength found in seclusion.
Creak of lone bamboo.

OF EMOTIONS

Within the complexities of withholding and so retaining any emotions concerning the personal self, it is a geisha's duty to portray their talent as the greatest of actors.

The control and constraint required in performing the utmost degree of limitation on wanted emotions to come forth is tackled with ease by an experienced geisha, a skill born from years of training. Yet such suppression of true emotions comes with a price.

To be filled with the joy and welcoming delight portrayed to each and every greeted client can at times stretch those whose duty it is to remain in such emotive states of being. This can leave a geisha depleted.

It is in this side effect often found in the appeasing of others that a geisha can succumb to scars of an emotional foundation. Wounds which in truth are no different to the deep callouses found on the end of delicate fingertips, a shamisen's taught strings to blame, bringing unwanted marks upon its instigator amid notes of beauty and compassion.

From experience, it was the betrayal of the true self which hindered the happiness and want of acceptance a practitioner of servitude to others secretly desires, yearnings of the soul which are shrouded in formality from the first moments of an apprentice's beginnings and into the following years of giehsahood with all its demands founded in correct display of ritual and tradition.

Although in such pitfalls of constant restraint and control over personal emotions there can be found a strength within itself. For is it not another talent tendered by those whose life is given to the pleasing of another, that the retaining of true sentiments remains hidden?

More so, it is in the realisation of such matters that leads an added air to surround a geisha's presence, giving an extra element of mystery and enticement to the bearer of veiled gifts.

Momoko of Gion

Beyond walled gardens,

the temples, the shrines,

solitary footsteps fall,

distinct in the click of wood on granite.

A dignified shuffle, the kimono's penance,

wrapped tight across slender frame,

a litheness enhanced beneath voluminous set hair,

its blackness reinforced against white powdered features.

Not a smile.

Sensibilities hidden.

Emotions of ardour and fervour kept secured within,

Unlocked only by those whose funds delight.

The Koi

Gentle in reflection

barren branches lay soft,

the pond's greeting held in slight ripples.

Eyed from below,

towards what was once cherry blossom pink,

a koi meanders,

those fragmented wooden veins the attraction.

A time of autumnal results

unconsidered amid now darkened scale...

no different to one housed in a kimono of finest silk.

In any setting,
so shall such feelings arrive,
from within the heart.

Ready, chapters new.
When or what shall be, will be.
Given. Completed.

About The Author

Born in Tokyo to a Japanese father and Italian mother, Elizabeth was raised in Japan until eight years old when her family then relocated to Switzerland.

Elizabeth returned to Japan at the age of twenty-one, where undertaking geisha training within the confines of Kyoto's Gion district, she became one of the few Eurasian women to live the life of a geisha until retiring at thirty-five years old.

Elizabeth now spends her time between Japan and Switzerland.

Printed in Great Britain
by Amazon

44226532R00067